Pope Francis on Eucharist

Pope Francis on Eucharist

100 Daily Meditations for Adoration, Prayer, and Reflection

Compiled by
John T. Kyler

Foreword by
Cardinal Blase J. Cupich

LITURGICAL PRESS
Collegeville, Minnesota

www.litpress.org

2	3	4	5	6	7	8	9

Library of Congress Cataloging-in-Publication Data

Names: Francis, Pope, 1936– author. | Kyler, John T., editor.
Title: Pope Francis on Eucharist : 100 daily meditations for adoration, prayer, and reflection / compiled by John T. Kyler.
Description: Collegeville, Minnesota : Liturgical Press, [2023] | Summary: "A collection of writings, homilies, and talks from Pope Francis, sharing a Eucharistic vision for the Church where all are fed and sustained by the Body of Christ"—Provided by publisher.
Identifiers: LCCN 2022030866 | ISBN 9780814668870 (trade paperback)
Subjects: LCSH: Lord's Supper—Catholic Church— Meditations. | Eucharistic prayers—Catholic Church.
Classification: LCC BX2169 .F73 2023 | DDC 234/.163— dc23/eng/20220908
LC record available at https://lccn.loc.gov/2022030866

Foreword

As the universal Church engages in a synodal process and as the Church in the United States fosters a Eucharistic revival, we are blessed to have this collection of Pope Francis's meditations on the Eucharist.

A synodal Church, as the two Greek words *syn* (with) and *hodos* (road) tell us, is the assembly of believers who walk on the road together with their Lord. And surely when we come together to celebrate the Eucharist, we are never more with the Lord and on the journey with him. As Pope Francis says, "[I]n the Eucharist the Lord makes us walk on his road" (Day 10).

As Pope Francis describes our experience of the Eucharist, he identifies that experience as deeply personal. We receive the Lord within us, and we meet him. And although that experience is deeply personal, it is never merely private. It does not just belong to us. He writes: "The Eucharist is not a sacrament 'for me'; it is the sacrament of the many, who form one body, God's holy and faithful people" (Day 11).

The intense personal and shared experience of the presence of the Lord in the Eucharist, as Pope Francis describes it, is also not a static or fixed presence. It is, we believe, real sacramental presence. And it is also a dynamic presence: we move with Jesus, and Jesus moves with us. Pope Francis says, "In the Eucharist Jesus . . . draws alongside us, pilgrims in history, to nourish the faith, hope and charity within us; to comfort us in trials, to sustain us in the commitment to justice and peace" (Day 65).

This personal, shared, and dynamic presence of the Lord finds echoes in one of the great Eucharistic hymns of our tradition, *Lauda Sion*, the sequence for the solemnity of Corpus Christi. In that hymn, we hear these memorable words:

> *Ecce, panis angelorum,*
> *Factus cibus viatorum:*
> *Vere panis filiorum . . .*

> Behold the Bread of angels,
> Become the food of travelers:
> Truly the bread of God's children . . .

Each time we encounter the Lord in his Eucharist, we rejoice to know that he is with us who have become sons and daughters in the Son. He is with us on the journey that leads one day to the heavenly banquet.

As you pick up Pope Francis's book of Eucharistic meditations, I hope that Pope Francis offers you a model for your prayer and encounter with the Eucharist. As you read his words, you will sense that he is doing what St. Thomas Aquinas described as *contemplata aliis tradere*, "handing on to others what we ourselves have contemplated." Like Pope Francis, may you be able to contemplate deeply the mystery of our

Eucharistic Lord in his dying and rising, in his faithful presence to us, and in the ways he accompanies us on the journey. From your contemplation, may you be able to share, especially with a younger generation, what the Eucharist means to you, so that more and more people can embrace this great gift.

Another hope that I have for you, as you consider Pope Francis's words, centers on the connection and unity that we have with each other in the Eucharist. We live in a time of fragmentation, and so many people feel divided from one another. Pope Francis keeps reminding us that we are—in the words of St. Francis of Assisi—*fratelli tutti*, "brothers and sisters to each other." The Eucharist is that strong center that holds us together. St. Paul wrote to the Corinthians: "The cup of blessing that we bless, is it not a sharing in the blood of Christ? The bread that we break, is it not a sharing in the body of Christ? Because there is one bread, we who are many are one body, for we all partake of the one bread" (1 Cor 10:16-17). May the Eucharist lead you to know the unity and connection that we have with each other, with the men and women of faith who have gone before us, and—one day—with all the saints in heaven.

Finally, I hope that your consideration of Pope Francis's meditations will lead you to claim your Eucharistic responsibility. What do I mean? The Eucharist, as action, presence, sign and source of unity, pledge of our future, is never just about our own betterment. The Eucharist propels us into mission, that is, to take responsibility for carrying the Lord into the world. After the two disciples on the road to

Emmaus encountered the Lord, and he shared God's Word with them and then broke his Eucharistic bread with them, St. Luke says, "That same hour they got up and returned to Jerusalem; and they found the eleven and their companions gathered together. . . . Then they told what had happened on the road, and how he had been made known to them in the breaking of the bread" (Luke 24:33, 35). From their experience of Eucharist, they claimed their responsibility to go in mission to share the Lord with others. May your reflections and prayers centered on the Eucharist lead you on the same path.

Cardinal Blase J. Cupich
Feast of Saint Francis
October 4, 2022

Day 1

The Eucharist communicates the Lord's love for us: a love so great that it nourishes us with Himself; a freely given love, always available to every person who hungers and needs to regenerate his own strength. To live the experience of faith means to allow oneself to be nourished by the Lord and to build one's own existence not with material goods but with the reality that does not perish: the gifts of God, his Word and his Body.

(Homily – June 19, 2014)

Day 2

To listen to Christ, in fact, entails *taking up the logic of his Pascal Mystery*, setting out on the journey with Him to make of oneself a gift of love to others, in docile obedience to the will of God, with an attitude of detachment from worldly things and of interior freedom.

(Angelus – March 1, 2015)

Day 3

In the Eucharist, we in fact encounter the living Jesus and His strength, and through Him we enter into communion with our brothers and sisters in the faith: those who live with us here on earth and those who have gone before us into the next life, the unending life. This reality fills us with joy: it is beautiful to have so many brothers and sisters in the faith who walk beside us, supporting us with their help, and together we travel the same road toward heaven. And it is comforting to know that there are other brothers and sisters who have already reached heaven, who await us and pray for us, so that together in eternity we can contemplate the glorious and merciful face of the Father.

(Angelus – November 1, 2014)

Day 4

We all go to Mass because we love Jesus and we want to share, through the Eucharist, in his passion and his resurrection. But do we love, as Jesus wishes, those brothers and sisters who are the most needy? For example, in Rome these days we have seen much social discomfort either due to the rain, which has caused so much damage to entire districts, or because of the lack of work, a consequence of the global economic crisis. I wonder, and each one of us should wonder: I who go to Mass, how do I live this? Do I try to help, to approach and pray for those in difficulty? Or am I a little indifferent?

(General Audience – February 12, 2014)

Day 5

If we look around, we realize that there are *so many offers of food* which do not come from the Lord and which appear to be more satisfying. Some nourish themselves with money, others with success and vanity, others with power and pride. But the food that truly nourishes and satiates us is only that which the Lord gives us!

(Homily – June 19, 2014)

Day 6

The bread of God is Jesus Himself. By receiving Him in Communion, we receive his life within us and we become children of the Heavenly Father and brothers and sisters among ourselves. By receiving communion we meet Jesus truly living and risen!

(Angelus – July 26, 2015)

Day 7

Adoration: that is the attitude we need in the presence of the Eucharist.

(Homily – June 6, 2021)

Day 8

Besides physical hunger, people experience another hunger, a hunger that cannot be satiated with ordinary food. It's a hunger for life, a hunger for love, a hunger for eternity.

(Homily – June 19, 2014)

Day 9

Nourishing ourselves of the Eucharistic Jesus also means abandoning ourselves trustingly to him and allowing ourselves to be guided by him. It means welcoming Jesus in place of one's own "me." In this way the love freely received from Jesus in the Eucharistic Communion, by the work of the Holy Spirit, nourishes our love for God and for the brothers and sisters we meet along the daily journey. Nourished by the Body of Christ, we become ever more concretely the mystical Body of Christ.

(Angelus – June 18, 2017)

Day 10

[I]n the Eucharist the Lord makes us walk on his road, that of service, of sharing, of giving; and if it is shared, that little we have, that little we are, becomes riches, for the power of God—which is the power of love—comes down into our poverty to transform it.

(Homily – May 30, 2013)

Day 11

The Eucharist also reminds us that we are not isolated individuals, but *one body*. As the people in the desert gathered the manna that fell from heaven and shared it in their families, so Jesus, the Bread come down from Heaven, calls us together to receive him and to share him with one another. The Eucharist is not a sacrament "for me"; it is the sacrament of the many, who form one body, God's holy and faithful people.

(Homily – June 18, 2017)

Day 12

Taking part in the Eucharist means entering into the logic of Jesus, the logic of giving freely, of sharing. And as poor as we are, we all have something to give. "To receive Communion" means to draw from Christ the grace which enables us to share with others all we are and all we have.

(Angelus – July 26, 2015)

Day 13

The Eucharist is at the heart of "Christian initiation," together with Baptism and Confirmation, and it constitutes the source of the Church's life itself. From this Sacrament of love, in fact, flows every authentic journey of faith, of communion and of witness.

(General Audience – February 5, 2014)

Day 14

There is always a Word of God that gives us guidance after we slip; and through our weariness and disappointments there is always a Bread that is broken that keeps us going on the journey.

(Regina Caeli – May 4, 2014)

Day 15

The world still does not know it, but everyone is invited to the supper of the wedding of the Lamb. To be admitted to the feast all that is required is the wedding garment of faith which comes from the hearing of his Word.

(*Desiderio Desideravi*, 5)

Day 16

The *bread* that Jesus teaches us to ask for
is what is necessary, not superfluous.
It is the bread of pilgrims, the righteous,
a bread that is neither accumulated nor
wasted, and that does not weigh us down
as we walk.

(Angelus – July 24, 2016)

Day 17

Through the Eucharist, the Lord also heals our *negative memory*, that negativity which seeps so often into our hearts. The Lord heals this negative memory, which drags to the surface things that have gone wrong and leaves us with the sorry notion that we are useless, that we only make mistakes, that we are ourselves a mistake. Jesus comes to tell us that this is not so. He wants to be close to us. Every time we receive him, he reminds us that we are precious, that we are guests he has invited to his banquet, friends with whom he wants to dine. And not only because he is generous, but because he is truly in love with us. He sees and loves the beauty and goodness that we are.

(Homily – June 14, 2020)

Day 18

[I]t is possible for each one of us to meet the Son of God, experiencing all of his love and infinite mercy. We are able to encounter Him truly present in the Sacraments, especially in the Eucharist. We are able to recognize Him in the faces of our brothers and sisters, especially in the poor, the sick, the imprisoned, the displaced: they are the living flesh of the suffering Christ and the visible image of the invisible God.

(Angelus – January 11, 2015)

Day 19

The Last Supper represents the culmination of Christ's entire life. It is not only the anticipation of his sacrifice which will be rendered on the Cross, but also the synthesis of a life offered for the salvation of the whole of humanity. Therefore, it is not enough to state that Jesus is present in the Eucharist, but one must see in it the presence of a life given and partake in it. When we take and eat that Bread, we are associated into the life of Jesus, we enter into communion with Him, we commit to achieve communion among ourselves, to transform our life into a gift, especially to the poorest.

(Angelus – June 7, 2015)

Day 20

[W]e become the Lord's tabernacles, carrying the Lord with us; to the point that he himself tells us: if we do not eat his body and drink his blood, we will not enter the kingdom of heaven.

(Homily – April 9, 2020)

Day 21

Nourishing ourselves of that "Bread of Life" means entering into harmony with the heart of Christ, assimilating his choices, his thoughts, his behavior.
It means entering into a dynamism of love and becoming people of peace, people of forgiveness, of reconciliation, of sharing in solidarity. The very things that Jesus did.

(Angelus – August 16, 2015)

Day 22

At the culmination of his life, [Jesus] does not distribute an abundance of bread to feed the multitudes, but breaks himself apart at the Passover supper with the disciples. In this way Jesus shows us that the aim of life lies in self-giving, that the greatest thing is to serve.

(Angelus – June 6, 2021)

Day 23

It is the Church that makes the Eucharist, but it is more fundamental that *the Eucharist makes the Church*, and allows her *to be her mission*, even before she accomplishes it. This is the mystery of communion, of the Eucharist: receiving Jesus so He may transform us from within, and receiving Jesus so that He may create unity in us and not division.

(Angelus – June 14, 2020)

Day 24

Let us pray that participation in the Eucharist may always be an incentive: to follow the Lord every day, to be instruments of communion and to share what we are with him and with our neighbor. Our life will then be truly fruitful.

(Homily – May 30, 2013)

Day 25

In our city that hungers for love and care, that suffers from decay and neglect, that contains so many elderly people living alone, families in difficulty, young people struggling to earn their bread and to realize their dreams, the Lord says to each one of you: "You yourself give them something to eat." You may answer: "But I have so little; I am not up to such things." That is not true; your "little" has great value in the eyes of Jesus, provided that you don't keep it to yourself, but put it in play. Put yourself in play! You are not alone, for you have the Eucharist, bread for the journey, the bread of Jesus.

(Homily – June 23, 2019)

Day 26

[I]n our fragmented lives, the Lord comes to meet us with a loving "fragility," which is the Eucharist. In the Bread of Life, the Lord comes to us, making himself a humble meal that lovingly heals our memory, wounded by life's frantic pace of life. The Eucharist is the *memorial of God's love*.

(Homily – June 18, 2017)

Day 27

At least once a day we find ourselves eating together; perhaps in the evening with our family, after a day of work or study. It would be lovely, before breaking bread, to invite Jesus, the bread of Life, to ask him simply to bless what we have done and what we have failed to do.
Let us invite him into our home; let us pray in a "homey" style. Jesus will be at the table with us and we will be fed by a greater love.

(Angelus – August 8, 2021)

Day 28

Jesus was broken; he is broken for us. And he asks us to give ourselves, to break ourselves, as it were, for others. This "breaking bread" became the icon, the sign for recognizing Christ and Christians.

(Homily – May 26, 2016)

Day 29

We should never forget that the Last Supper of Jesus took place "on the night he was betrayed" (1 Cor 11:23). In the bread and in the wine which we offer and around which we gather, the gift of Christ's body and blood is renewed every time for the remission of our sins.
We must go to Mass humbly, like sinners and the Lord reconciles us.

(General Audience – February 12, 2014)

Day 30

God knows how difficult it is, he knows
how weak our memory is, and he has
done something remarkable: he left us a
memorial. He did not just leave us words,
for it is easy to forget what we hear.
He did not just leave us the Scriptures,
for it is easy to forget what we read.
He did not just leave us signs, for we can
forget even what we see. He gave us
Food, for it is not easy to forget something we have actually tasted. He left us
Bread in which he is truly present, alive
and true, with all the flavor of his love.
Receiving him we can say: "He is the
Lord; he remembers me!" That is why
Jesus told us: "Do this in remembrance
of me" (1 Cor 11:24).

(Homily – June 14, 2020)

Day 31

The Eucharist gives us a *grateful* memory, because it makes us see that we are the Father's children, whom he loves and nourishes. It gives us a *free* memory, because Jesus' love and forgiveness heal the wounds of the past, soothe our remembrance of wrongs experienced and inflicted. It gives us a *patient* memory, because amid all our troubles we know that the Spirit of Jesus remains in us.

(Homily – June 18, 2017)

Day 32

Jesus, Bread of eternal life, came down from heaven and was made flesh thanks to the faith of Mary Most Holy. After having borne him with ineffable love in herself, she followed him faithfully unto the Cross and to the resurrection. Let us ask Our Lady to help us rediscover the beauty of the Eucharist, to make it the center of our life, especially at Sunday Mass and in adoration.

(Angelus – June 22, 2014)

Day 33

The Bread of Life, in fact, heals rigidity and transforms it into docility. The Eucharist heals because it unites with Jesus: it makes us assimilate his way of living, his ability to break himself apart and give himself to brothers and sisters, to respond to evil with good. He gives us the courage to go outside of ourselves and bend down with love toward the fragility of others. As God does with us.

(Angelus – June 6, 2021)

Day 34

The food the Lord offers us is different from other food, and perhaps it doesn't seem as flavorful to us as certain other dishes the world offers us. So we dream of other dishes, like the Hebrews in the desert, who longed for the meat and onions they ate in Egypt, but forgot that they had eaten those meals at the table of slavery.

(Homily – June 19, 2014)

Day 35

Sharing the word and celebrating the Eucharist together fosters fraternity and makes us a holy and missionary community. It also gives rise to authentic and shared mystical experiences.

(*Gaudete et Exsultate*, 142)

Day 36

We should not grow accustomed to the Eucharist and go to Communion as a habit: no! Each time we approach the altar to receive the Eucharist, we must truly renew our "amen" to the Body of Christ. When the priest says "the Body of Christ," we say "amen": but let it be an "amen" that comes from the heart, a committed one. It is Jesus; it is Jesus who saved me; it is Jesus who comes to give me the strength to live. It is Jesus, the living Jesus. But we must not become accustomed: each time as if it were the first Communion.

(Angelus – June 23, 2019)

All that we have in the world does not satisfy our infinite hunger. We need Jesus, to be with him, to be nourished at his table, on his words of eternal life! Believing in Jesus means making him the center, the meaning of our life. Christ is not an optional element: he is the "Living Bread," the essential nourishment. Binding oneself to him, in a true relationship of faith and love, does not mean being tied down, but being profoundly free, always on the journey.

(Angelus – August 23, 2015)

Day 38

[W]e don't ever thank [the] Lord enough for the gift he has given us in the Eucharist! It is a very great gift and that is why it is so important to go to Mass on Sunday. Go to Mass not just to pray, but to receive Communion, the bread that is the Body of Jesus Christ who saves us, forgives us, unites us to the Father. It is a beautiful thing to do! And we go to Mass every Sunday because that is the day of the resurrection of the Lord. That is why Sunday is so important to us. And in this Eucharist we feel this belonging to the Church, to the People of God, to the Body of God, to Jesus Christ. We will never completely grasp the value and the richness of it. Let us ask him then that this Sacrament continue to keep his presence alive in the Church and to shape our community in charity and communion, according to the Father's heart.

(General Audience – February 5, 2014)

Day 39

God makes himself tiny, like a morsel of bread. That is precisely why we need a great heart to be able to recognize, adore and receive him. God's presence is so humble, hidden and often unseen that, in order to recognize his presence, we need a heart that is ready, alert and welcoming. But if our heart, rather than a large room, is more like a closet where we wistfully keep things from the past, or an attic where we long ago stored our dreams and enthusiasm, or a dreary chamber filled only with us, our problems and our disappointments, then it will be impossible to recognize God's silent and unassuming presence.

(Homily – June 6, 2021)

Day 40

This is why the Eucharistic commemoration does us so much good: it is not an abstract, cold and superficial memory, but a living remembrance that comforts us with God's love. A memory that is both recollection and imitation. The Eucharist is flavored with Jesus' words and deeds, the taste of his Passion, the fragrance of his Spirit. When we receive it, our hearts are overcome with the certainty of Jesus' love.

(Homily – June 18, 2017)

Day 41

In the Eucharist fragility is strength: the strength of the love that becomes small so it can be welcomed and not feared; the strength of the love that is broken and shared so as to nourish and give life; the strength of the love that is split apart so as to join all of us in unity.

(Angelus – June 6, 2021)

Day 42

Jesus takes the bread in his hands and says "Take; this is my body" (Mk 14:22). With this gesture and with these words, He assigns to the bread a function which is no longer simply that of physical nutrition, but that of making his Person present in the midst of the community of believers.

(Angelus – June 7, 2015)

Day 43

It is noteworthy how close the link is between the Eucharistic bread, nourishment for eternal life, and daily bread, necessary for earthly life. Before offering Himself to the Father as the Bread of salvation, Jesus ensures there is food for those who follow Him and who, in order to be with Him, forgot to make provisions.

(Angelus – August 2, 2020)

Day 44

The Eucharist is the sacrament of communion that brings us out of individualism so that we may follow him together, living out our faith in him. Therefore we should all ask ourselves before the Lord: how do I live the Eucharist? Do I live it anonymously or as a moment of true communion with the Lord, and also with all the brothers and sisters who share this same banquet? What are our Eucharistic celebrations like?

(Homily – May 30, 2013)

Day 45

Jesus prepares *a place* for us *here below*, because the Eucharist is the beating heart of the Church. It gives her birth and rebirth; it gathers her together and gives her strength. But the Eucharist also prepares for us *a place on high*, in eternity, for it is the *Bread of heaven*. It comes down from heaven—it is the only matter on earth that savors of eternity. It is the bread of things to come; even now, it grants us a foretaste of a future infinitely greater than all we can hope for or imagine. It is the bread that sates our greatest expectations and feeds our finest dreams. It is, in a word, the *pledge* of eternal life—not simply a promise but a pledge, a concrete anticipation of what awaits us there.

(Homily – June 3, 2018)

Day 46

The Eucharist is the summit of God's saving action: the Lord Jesus, by becoming bread broken for us, pours upon us all of his mercy and his love, so as to renew our hearts, our lives and our way of relating with him and with all. It is for this reason that commonly, when we approach this Sacrament, we speak of "receiving Communion," of "taking Communion": this means that by the power of the Holy Spirit, participation in Holy Communion conforms us in a singular and profound way to Christ, giving us a foretaste already now of the full communion with the Father that characterizes the heavenly banquet, where together with all the Saints we will have the joy of contemplating God face to face.

(General Audience – February 5, 2014)

Day 47

The Eucharist is the culmination of Jesus'
entire life, which was a single act of love
toward the Father and brothers and
sisters. There too, as with the miracle of
the multiplication of the loaves, Jesus
took the bread in his hands, raised a
prayer of blessing to the Father, broke
the bread and gave it to his disciples;
and he did the same with the cup of wine.
But in that moment, on the eve of his
Passion, with that gesture, he wished to
leave the Testament of his new and
eternal Covenant, a perpetual memorial
of the Paschal Mystery of his death and
resurrection.

(Angelus – June 23, 2019)

Day 48

To celebrate the Eucharist, we need first to recognize our thirst for God, to sense our need for him, to long for his presence and love, to realize that we cannot go it alone, but need the Food and Drink of eternal life to sustain us on our journey. The tragedy of the present time—we can say—is that this thirst is felt less and less. Questions about God are no longer asked, desire for God has faded, seekers of God have become increasingly rare. God no longer attracts us because we no longer acknowledge our deep thirst for him.

(Homily – June 6, 2021)

Day 49

[T]he Eucharistic Celebration is much more than simple banquet: it is exactly the memorial of Jesus' Paschal Sacrifice, the mystery at the center of salvation. "Memorial" does not simply mean a remembrance, a mere memory; it means that every time we celebrate this Sacrament we participate in the mystery of the passion, death and resurrection of Christ.

(General Audience – February 5, 2014)

Day 50

Jesus, then, prepares for us and asks us to be prepared. What does Jesus prepare for us? He prepares *a place and a meal*. A place much more worthy than the "large furnished room" of the Gospel. It is our spacious and vast home here below, the Church, where there is, and must be, room for everyone. But he has also reserved a place for us on high, in heaven, so that we can be with him and with one another for ever. In addition to a place, he prepares a meal, the Bread in which he gives himself: "Take; this is my body" (Mk 14:22). These two gifts, a place and a meal, are what we need to live. They are our ultimate "room and board." Both are bestowed upon us in the Eucharist. A place and a meal.

(Homily – June 3, 2018)

Day 51

With this gesture, Jesus demonstrates His power; not in a spectacular way but as a sign of charity, of God the Father's generosity toward His weary and needy children. He is immersed in the life of His people, He understands their fatigue and their limitations, but He does not allow anyone to be lost, or to lose out: He nourishes them with His word and provides food in plenty for sustenance.

(Angelus – August 2, 2020)

Day 52

Do! The Eucharist is not simply an act of remembrance; it is a *fact*: the Lord's Passover is made present once again for us. In Mass the death and resurrection of Jesus are set before us. *Do this in remembrance of me*: come together and celebrate the Eucharist as a community, as a people, as a family, in order to remember me. We cannot do without the Eucharist, for it is God's memorial. And it heals our wounded memory.

(Homily – June 14, 2020)

Day 53

Today is the day to ask, ". . . Do I, who have so often been fed by the Body of Jesus, make any effort to relieve the hunger of the poor?" Let us not remain indifferent. Let us not live *a one-way faith*, a faith that receives but does not give, a faith that accepts the gift but does not give it in return. Having received mercy, let us now become merciful. For if love is only about us, faith becomes arid, barren and sentimental. Without others, faith becomes disembodied.

(Homily – April 11, 2021)

Day 54

Jesus became bread broken for our sake; in turn, he asks us to give ourselves to others, to live no longer for ourselves but *for one another*. In this way, we live "eucharistically," pouring out upon the world the love we draw from the Lord's flesh. The Eucharist is translated into life when we pass *beyond ourselves to those all around us*.

(Homily – June 3, 2018)

Day 55

Thanks to Jesus and to his Spirit, even our life becomes "bread broken" for our brothers and sisters. And living like this we discover true joy! The joy of making of oneself a gift, of reciprocating the great gift that we have first received, without merit of our own. This is beautiful: our life is made a gift! This is to imitate Jesus.

(Angelus – June 22, 2014)

Day 56

We are a community nourished by the body and blood of Christ. Communion with the body of Christ is an effective sign of unity, of communion, of sharing. One cannot participate in the Eucharist without committing oneself to mutual fraternity, which is sincere. But the Lord knows well that our human strength alone is not enough for this. On the contrary, He knows that among His disciples there will always be the temptation of rivalry, envy, prejudice, division. . . . We are all aware of these things. For this reason too He left us the Sacrament of His real, tangible and permanent Presence, so that, in remaining united to him, we may always receive the gift of fraternal love. "Abide in my love" (Jn 15:9), Jesus said; and this is possible thanks to the Eucharist. To abide in friendship, in love.

(Angelus – June 14, 2020)

Day 57

Each time we receive the Bread of Life, Jesus comes to give new meaning to our fragilities. He reminds us that in his eyes we are more precious than we think.
He tells us he is pleased if we share our fragilities with him. He repeats to us that his mercy is not afraid of our miseries. The mercy of Jesus is not afraid of our miseries. And above all he heals us from those fragilities that we cannot heal on our own, with love.

(Angelus – June 6, 2021)

Day 58

How many mothers, how many fathers, together with the slices of bread they provide each day on the tables of their homes, have broken their hearts to let their children grow, and grow well! How many Christians, as responsible citizens, have broken their own lives to defend the dignity of all, especially the poorest, the marginalized and those discriminated! Where do they find the strength to do this? It is in the Eucharist: in the power of the Risen Lord's love, who today too breaks bread for us and repeats: "Do this in remembrance of me."

(Homily – May 26, 2016)

Day 59

Jesus leaves us the Eucharist as the Church's daily remembrance of, and deeper sharing in, the event of his Passover (cf. Lk 22:19). The joy of evangelizing always arises from grateful remembrance: it is a grace which we constantly need to implore.

(*Evangelii Gaudium*, 13)

Day 60

Jesus' gesture at the Last Supper is the ultimate thanksgiving to the Father for his love, for his mercy. "Thanksgiving" in Greek is expressed as "eucharist." And that is why the Sacrament is called the Eucharist: it is the supreme thanksgiving to the Father, who so loved us that he gave us his Son out of love. This is why the term Eucharist includes the whole of that act, which is the act of God and humanity together, the act of Jesus Christ, true God and true Man.

(General Audience – February 5, 2014)

Day 61

We must always bear in mind that the Eucharist is not something we make; it [is] not our own commemoration of what Jesus said and did. No. It is precisely an act of Christ! It is Christ who acts there, who is on the altar. It is a gift of Christ, who makes himself present and gathers us around him, to nourish us with his Word and with his life. This means that the mission and the very identity of the Church flows from there, from the Eucharist, and there always takes its shape.

(General Audience – February 12, 2014)

Day 62

Let us break the bread of our lives in compassion and solidarity, so that through us the world may see the grandeur of God's love. Then the Lord will come, he will surprise us once more, he will again become food for the life of the world. And he will satisfy us always, until the day when, at the heavenly banquet, we will contemplate his face and come to know the joy that has no end.

(Homily – June 6, 2021)

Day 63

The Eucharist heals *orphaned memory*. So many people have memories marked by a lack of affection and bitter disappointments caused by those who should have given them love and instead orphaned their hearts. We would like to go back and change the past, but we cannot. God, however, can heal these wounds by placing within our memory a greater love: his own love. The Eucharist brings us the Father's faithful love, which heals our sense of being orphans. It gives us Jesus' love, which transformed a tomb from an end to a beginning, and in the same way can transform our lives. It fills our hearts with the consoling love of the Holy Spirit, who never leaves us alone and always heals our wounds.

(Homily – June 14, 2020)

Day 64

Jesus' living presence in the Eucharist is like a door, an open door between the temple and the road, between faith and history, between the city of God and the city of humanity.

(Angelus – June 3, 2018)

Day 65

In the Eucharist Jesus, as he did with the disciples at Emmaus, draws alongside us, pilgrims in history, to nourish the faith, hope and charity within us; to comfort us in trials; to sustain us in the commitment to justice and peace. This supportive presence of the Son of God is everywhere: in cities and the countryside, in the North and South of the world, in countries with a Christian tradition and in those newly evangelized. In the Eucharist he offers himself as spiritual strength so as to help us put into practice his commandment—to love one another as he loved us—building communities that are welcoming and open to the needs of all, especially the most frail, poor and needy people.

(Angelus – June 18, 2017)

Day 66

May our prayer sustain the common commitment that no one may lack the heavenly Bread which gives eternal life and the basic necessities for a dignified life, and may it affirm the logic of sharing and love.

(Angelus – July 26, 2015)

Day 67

Don't forget these two things: the measure of the love of God is love without measure. And following Jesus, we, with the Eucharist, make of our life a gift.

(Angelus – June 22, 2014)

Day 68

What does *bread of life* mean? We need bread to live. Those who are hungry do not ask for refined and expensive food, they ask for bread. Those who are unemployed do not ask for enormous wages, but the "bread" of employment. Jesus reveals himself as bread, that is, the essential, what is necessary for everyday life; without Him it does not work. Not *one* bread among many others, but *the* bread of life. In other words, without him, rather than living, we get by: because he alone nourishes the soul; he alone forgives us from that evil that we cannot overcome on our own; he alone makes us feel loved even if everyone else disappoints us; he alone gives us the strength to love and, he alone gives us the strength to forgive in difficulties; he alone gives that peace to the heart that it is searching for; he alone gives eternal life when life here on earth ends. He is the essential bread of life.

(Angelus – August 8, 2021)

Day 69

The Eucharist is the *sacrament of unity*. Whoever receives it cannot fail to be a builder of unity, because building unity has become part of his or her "spiritual DNA." May this *Bread of unity* heal our ambition to lord it over others, to greedily hoard things for ourselves, to foment discord and criticism. May it awaken in us the joy of living in love, without rivalry, jealousy or mean-spirited gossip.

(Homily – June 18, 2017)

Day 70

The Lord, offering himself to us in the simplicity of bread, also invites us not to waste our lives in chasing the myriad illusions that we think we cannot do without, yet that leave us empty within.
The Eucharist satisfies our hunger for material things and kindles our desire to serve. It raises us from our comfortable and lazy lifestyle and reminds us that we are not only mouths to be fed, but also his hands, to be used to help feed others. It is especially urgent now to take care of those who hunger for food and for dignity, of those without work and those who struggle to carry on. And this we must do in a real way, as real as the Bread that Jesus gives us. Genuine closeness is needed, as are true bonds of solidarity. In the Eucharist, Jesus draws close to us: let us not turn away from those around us!

(Homily – June 14, 2020)

Day 71

In the Eucharist, we contemplate and worship the God of love. The Lord who breaks no one, yet allows himself to be broken. The Lord who does not demand sacrifices, but sacrifices himself. The Lord who asks nothing but gives everything. In celebrating and experiencing the Eucharist, we too are called to share in this love.

(Homily – June 6, 2021)

Day 72

Everyone can share in some way in the life of the Church; everyone can be part of the community, nor should the doors of the sacraments be closed for simply any reason. . . . The Eucharist, although it is the fullness of sacramental life, is not a prize for the perfect but a powerful medicine and nourishment for the weak.

(*Evangelii Gaudium*, 47)

Day 73

The Eucharist is our "reservation" for the heavenly banquet; it is Jesus himself, as food for our journey towards eternal life and happiness.

(Homily – June 3, 2018)

Day 74

Indeed the Eucharist is itself an act of cosmic love: "Yes, cosmic! Because even when it is celebrated on the humble altar of a country church, the Eucharist is always in some way celebrated on the altar of the world." The Eucharist joins heaven and earth; it embraces and penetrates all creation. The world which came forth from God's hands returns to him in blessed and undivided adoration: in the bread of the Eucharist, "creation is projected towards divinization, towards the holy wedding feast, towards unification with the Creator himself." Thus, the Eucharist is also a source of light and motivation for our concerns for the environment, directing us to be stewards of all creation.

(*Laudato Si'*, 236)

Day 75

Indeed in [the Eucharist] we contemplate Jesus, Bread broken and offered, Blood poured out for our salvation. It is a presence which like fire sears the selfish attitudes within us, purifies us of the tendency to give only when we have received, and ignites the desire to make ourselves too, in union with Christ, bread broken and blood poured out for our brothers and sisters.

(Angelus – June 3, 2018)

Day 76

Meeting and welcoming within us Jesus, "Bread of Life," gives meaning and hope to the often winding journey of life. This "Bread of Life" is given to us with a task, namely, that we in our turn satisfy the spiritual and material hunger of our brothers and sisters, proclaiming the Gospel the world over.

(Angelus – August 2, 2015)

Day 77

The Christ, who nourishes us under the consecrated species of bread and wine, is the same One who comes to us in the everyday happenings; He is in the poor person who holds out his hand, in the suffering one who begs for help, in the brother or sister who asks for our availability and awaits our welcome. He is in the child who knows nothing about Jesus or salvation, who does not have faith. He is in every human being, even the smallest and the defenseless.

(Angelus – June 7, 2015)

Day 78

Don't forget these two things: the measure of the love of God is love without measure. And following Jesus, we, with the Eucharist, make of our life a gift.

(Angelus – June 22, 2014)

For us a vague memory of the Last Supper
would do no good. We need to be present
at that Supper, to be able to hear his voice,
to eat his Body and to drink his Blood.
We need Him. In the Eucharist and in all
the sacraments we are guaranteed the
possibility of encountering the Lord Jesus
and of having the power of his Paschal
Mystery reach us. The salvific power of
the sacrifice of Jesus, his every word,
his every gesture, glance, and feeling
reaches us through the celebration of
the sacraments.

(*Desiderio Desideravi*, 11)

Day 80

[T]he Eucharist is not a private prayer or a beautiful spiritual exercise, it is not a simple commemoration of what Jesus did at the Last Supper. We say, in order to fully understand, that the Eucharist is "a remembrance," that is, a gesture which renders real and present the event of Jesus' death and resurrection: the bread really is his Body given up for us, the wine really is his Blood poured out for us.

(Angelus – August 16, 2015)

Day 81

The Sacraments are a privileged way in which nature is taken up by God to become a means of mediating supernatural life. . . . For Christians, all the creatures of the material universe find their true meaning in the incarnate Word, for the Son of God has incorporated in his person part of the material world, planting in it a seed of definitive transformation.

(*Laudato Si'*, 235)

Day 82

We, today, may ask ourselves: what about me? *Where do I want to eat?* At which table [do] I want to be nourished? At the Lord's table? Or do I dream about eating flavorful foods, but in slavery? Moreover, we may ask ourselves: what do I recall? The Lord who saves me, or the garlic and onions of slavery? Which recollection satiates my soul?

(Homily – June 19, 2014)

"Do this." That is, take bread, give thanks and break it; take the chalice, give thanks, and share it. Jesus gives the command to *repeat this action* by which he instituted the memorial of his own Pasch, and in so doing gives us his Body and his Blood. This action reaches us today: it is the "doing" of the Eucharist which always has Jesus as its subject, but which is made real through our poor hands anointed by the Holy Spirit.

(Homily – May 26, 2016)

Let us not forget that the Eucharist is meant to nourish those who are weary and hungry along the way. A Church of the pure and perfect is a room with no place for anyone. On the other hand, a Church with open doors, that gathers and celebrates around Christ, is a large room where everyone—everyone, the righteous and sinners—can enter.

(Homily – June 6, 2021)

Day 85

The Eucharist is also the great sacrament that signifies and realizes the Church's *unity*. It is celebrated "so that from being strangers, dispersed and indifferent to each another, we may become united, equals and friends."

(*Querida Amazonia*, 91)

Day 86

The Eucharist, source of love for the life of the Church, is the school of charity and solidarity. Those who are nourished by the Bread of Christ cannot remain indifferent to those who do not have their daily bread.

(Angelus – June 7, 2015)

Day 87

In this way the Eucharist fosters a mature Christian lifestyle. The charity of Christ, welcomed with an open heart, changes us, transforms us, renders us capable of loving not according to human measure, always limited, but according to the measure of God. And what is the measure of God? Without measure! The measure of God is without measure. Everything! Everything! Everything! It's impossible to measure the love of God: it is without measure! And so we become capable of loving even those who do not love us: and this is not easy.

(Angelus – June 22, 2014)

Day 88

Any offense or wound or violence to the body of our neighbor is an affront to God the Creator! My thoughts go, in particular, to the children, the women, the elderly who are physically abused. In the flesh of these people we find the Body of Christ. Christ wounded, mocked, slandered, humiliated, scourged, crucified. . . . Jesus taught us love. A love that, in his Resurrection, is demonstrated to be more powerful than sin and death, and seeks to redeem all those who experience in their own body the slavery of our time.

(Regina Caeli – April 15, 2018)

Day 89

This is the logic of the Eucharist: we receive Jesus who loves us and heals our fragilities in order to love others and help them in their fragilities; and this lasts our entire life.

(Angelus – June 6, 2021)

Day 90

We turn to Him with faith: Jesus, defend us from the temptation of worldly food which enslaves us, tainted food; purify our memory, so it isn't imprisoned in selfish and worldly selectivity, but that it may be a *living memory of your presence* throughout the history of your people, a memory that makes a "monument" of your gesture of redeeming love.

(Homily – June 19, 2014)

Day 91

The Eucharist encourages us: even on the roughest road, we are not alone; the Lord does not forget us and whenever we turn to him, he restores us with his love.

(Homily – June 18, 2017)

Day 92

The Lord does great things with our littleness, as he did with the five loaves. He does not work spectacular miracles or wave a magic wand; he works with simple things. God's omnipotence is lowly, made up of love alone. And love can accomplish great things with little. The Eucharist teaches us this: for there we find God himself contained in a piece of bread. Simple, essential, bread broken and shared, the Eucharist we receive allows us to see things as God does. It inspires us to give ourselves to others. It is the antidote to the mindset that says: "Sorry, that is not my problem," or: "I have no time, I can't help you, it's none of my business." Or that looks the other way . . .

(Homily – June 23, 2019)

Day 93

We who go to Mass can ask: What is it that we bring to the world? Is it our sadness and bitterness, or the joy of the Lord? Do we receive Holy Communion and then carry on complaining, criticizing and feeling sorry for ourselves? This does not improve anything, whereas the joy of the Lord can change lives.

(Homily – June 14, 2020)

Day 94

[W]e cannot break bread on Sunday if our hearts are closed to our brothers and sisters. We cannot partake of that Bread if we do not give bread to the hungry. We cannot share that Bread unless we share the sufferings of our brothers and sisters in need. In the end, and the end of our solemn Eucharistic liturgies as well, only love will remain. Even now, our Eucharistic celebrations are transforming the world to the extent that we are allowing ourselves to be transformed and to become bread broken for others.

(Homily – June 6, 2021)

Day 95

In the Eucharist, Christ is always renewing his gift of self, which he made on the Cross. His whole life is an act of total sharing of self out of love; thus, he loved to be with his disciples and with the people whom he had a chance to know. This meant for him sharing in their aspirations, their problems, what stirred their soul and their life. Now we, when participating in Holy Mass, we find ourselves with all sorts of men and women: young people, the elderly, children; poor and well-off; locals and strangers alike; people with their families and people who are alone. . . . But the Eucharist which I celebrate, does it lead me to truly feel they are all like brothers and sisters? Does it increase my capacity to rejoice with those who are rejoicing and cry with those who are crying? Does it urge me to go out to the poor, the sick, the marginalized? Does it help me to recognize in theirs the face of Jesus?

(General Audience – February 12, 2014)

Day 96

[W]hat is meant by "eat the flesh and drink the blood" of Jesus? Is it just an image, a figure of speech, a symbol, or does it indicate something real? In order to answer, one must divine what is happening in Jesus' heart as he breaks the bread for the hungry crowd. Knowing that he will have to die on the cross for us, Jesus identifies himself with that bread broken and shared, and it becomes for him the "sign" of the Sacrifice that awaits him. This process culminates in the Last Supper, where the bread and wine *truly become his Body and his Blood.*

(Angelus – August 16, 2015)

Do not forget: Gospel, Eucharist, Prayer. Thanks to these gifts of the Lord we are able to conform not to the world but to Christ, and follow him on his path, the path of "losing one's life" in order to find it (Mt 16:25). "To lose it" in the sense of giving it, offering it through love and in love—and this leads to sacrifice, also the cross—to receive it liberated from selfishness and from the mortgage of death, newly purified, full of eternity.

(Angelus – August 31, 2014)

Day 98

Jesus is present in the sacrament of the Eucharist to be our nourishment, to be assimilated and to become in us that renewing force that gives once again the energy and gives once more the desire to set out again after every pause or after every fall. But this requires our consent, our willingness to let ourselves, our way of thinking and acting, be transformed. Otherwise the Eucharistic celebrations in which we participate are reduced to empty and formal rituals. Often some go to Mass because they have to go, as if it were a social event, respectful but social. However, the mystery is something else. It is Jesus who is present and comes to nourish us.

(Angelus – June 14, 2020)

Day 99

Jesus prepares for us *a meal*, food for our nourishment. In life, we constantly need to be fed: nourished not only with food, but also with plans and affection, hopes and desires. We hunger to be loved. But the most pleasing compliments, the finest gifts and the most advanced technologies are not enough; they never completely satisfy us. The Eucharist is simple food, like bread, yet it is the only food that satisfies, for *there is no greater love*.

(Homily – June 3, 2018)

Day 100

A celebration may be flawless on the exterior, very beautiful, but if it does not lead us to encounter Jesus Christ, it is unlikely to bear any kind of nourishment to our heart and our life. Through the Eucharist, however, Christ wishes to enter into our life and permeate it with his grace, so that in every Christian community there may be coherence between liturgy and life.

(General Audience – February 12, 2014)